THE CRAZY CAREERS OF VIDEO GAME DESIGNERS

ARIE KAPLAN

Lerner Publications Company • Minneapolis

Lerner Publications Company
A division of Lerner Publishing Group, Inc.
241 First Avenue North
Minneapolis, MN 55401 U.S.A.

Website address: www.lernerbooks.com

Content Consultant: Crystle Martin, postdoctoral researcher, Digital Media and Learning Hub at the University of California, Irvine

Library of Congress Cataloging-in-Publication Data

Kaplan, Arie.
    The crazy careers of video game designers / by Arie Kaplan.
        pages cm. — (Shockzone—games and gamers)
    Includes index.
    ISBN 978-1-4677-1249-1 (lib. bdg. : alk. paper)
    ISBN 978-1-4677-1782-3 (eBook)
    1. Video games—Design—Vocational guidance. 2. Video games industry—Vocational guidance. I. Title.
GV1469.3.K34 2014
794.8—dc23
                                                                        2013001161

Manufactured in the United States of America
1 – MG – 7/15/13

TABLE OF CONTENTS

FROM PLAYING HARD TO WORKING HARD

If you love video games, you might think making them would be **the ultimate dream job.** And if you're passionate and creative, it'd definitely be a great way to make a living. However, don't go thinking it's all just fun and games. Careers in the video game industry require lots of studying, reading, and work. You need to not just play hard, but work hard too.

You may love playing video games. But have you ever considered making them?

Still interested? Good. Let's check out the crazy careers you can find in the game industry. Do you like writing stories? Writing game scripts might be right up your alley. Maybe you keep a sketchbook in your backpack. If so, you might enjoy being an environment or character artist. If you enjoy working with computers, a career in programming, animating, or rigging might be for you. But what do people in these jobs actually do? Keep reading to find out.

Game maker James Silva works for a two-person company.

INDIE GAME COMPANIES

At huge game companies like Nintendo and Sony, you'll find tons of people doing the different jobs profiled in this book. New *Super Mario* or *Call of Duty* games might involve dozens of programmers and artists. But not all games are made this way. Indie (independent) game companies are sometimes one-person operations. One person has to do all the different jobs at the same time. So working at an indie game company can be a bit like juggling 10 balls at once.

GAME DESIGNER:
The Grand Planner

Think about the following people. The coach. The orchestra conductor. The boss. What do they have in common? DING! Time's up. That's right: they are all leaders. And just as teams, orchestras, and offices need leaders, so do video games. The game designer's job combines the responsibilities of all three leaders into one. Like the coach, the designer has to figure out the overall game plan. Like the orchestra conductor, the designer makes sure everyone working on the game is in sync. And like the boss, the designer ensures everyone is doing the job properly.

When a company decides to make a game, the game designer is the first person called in. She or he plans nearly everything in the game. This could include the story line, the characters, and the levels. The designer decides how the game will look and how players will control it.

A game designer's specific jobs can change depending on the game. Still, one thing always remains the same. It's the designer's job to make sure that the game is fun for players. The designer gives directions to the artists, the animators, and the programmers. If the directions are good, the game could be a classic. But if the directions are bad, it could end up being an epic fail.

VIDEO GAME CAREER MAP

The people who make games have to work together to make great ones. The result can get pretty messy pretty quickly. Just check out this map showing the connections between the careers in this book. No wonder the game designer has to be a master organizer.

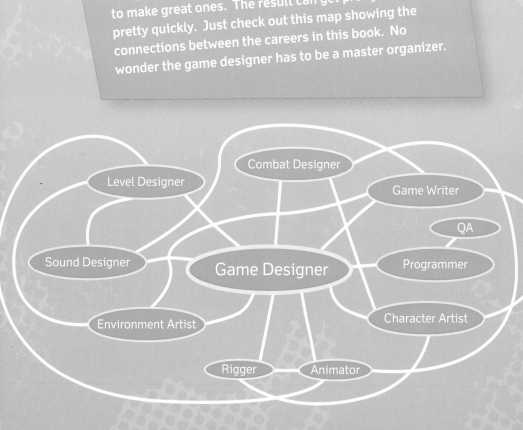

- Combat Designer
- Level Designer
- Game Writer
- QA
- Sound Designer
- Game Designer
- Programmer
- Environment Artist
- Character Artist
- Rigger
- Animator

LEVEL DESIGNER:
Where Are We Going?

The level designer is like a travel agent with infinite power. He or she decides where and when the game takes place. The designer can transport gamers to any time and place imaginable. Want to walk through a crowded plaza in 15th-century Italy? No problem. Sneak into an alien spaceship in the distant future? Easy as pie. Make the game-winning catch in the middle of a packed sports stadium? Got it.

The level designer also figures out where the characters can and can't go. Think of a game set in a vast jungle. You can't have the player just wandering off in the wrong direction. You want the characters to find the tomb filled with treasure—not the pit of jaguars. (Although on second thought, maybe you do.) The designer has to figure out a way to guide players in the right direction. By making these barriers hidden, they keep gamers immersed in the game world.

Level designers also decide where to put characters, vehicles, and other objects. They make the levels fun for players while keeping true to the game designer's overall plan. Making the game interesting often means coming up with more than one path through a level. For example, if players open door A, they find a pot of gold. But if they open door B, they encounter a fire-breathing dragon. (Hint: don't open door B.) Having lots of level paths makes players feel as if they have more control over the game.

Level designers must also come up with level objectives. These are the tasks a player must do to beat each level. Do they have to search for a priceless treasure? Escape from a crowd of zombies? Steal a scientific gadget? Or maybe all of the above? Hmm . . . sounds like a fun game.

Level designers must make game worlds both interesting and easy to explore.

MAGDEBVRG, ANNO 1207

COMBAT DESIGNER:
Everyone Behave!

COMBAT DESIGNER:
Everyone Behave!

Imagine if, as part of your job, you had to decide between a powerful punch and a magical fireball attack. Well, that's pretty much the job description for combat designer. This person figures out how game characters will battle one another. After the level designer decides where characters will travel in the level, the combat designer puts enemies in their way to make the journey more difficult. For example, imagine the heroine is in a dark, damp sewer. The combat designer might put giant rats fierce alligators, and screeching bats in her path. The combat designer would also decide how the enemies would attack her. The rats might bite at the heroine's ankles. The gators might whip with their tails. The bats might swarm to block her path.

The combat designer also decides how the heroine will fight back. She could throw cheese to distract the rats. She could kick water into the gators' eyes and shine a flashlight at the bats to make them scatter. The combat designer works with the level and game designers to make sure everything fits together.

Combat design can often be a team effort.

GAME WRITER:
Tell Me a Story

You arrive at work. After grabbing coffee and a doughnut, you sit down at your desk. You open up your toolbox. Looking inside, you see that it contains everything in the universe. Whoa. This is basically what being a game writer is like. You can write anything in your games that you can imagine.

Like any other kind of writer, a video game writer's job is to tell an amazing story. But game scripts contain things that aren't found in other kinds of storytelling. As the player makes choices, a game's story can go in different directions, or branches.

In a game where a medieval king asks you to go on a quest, you could accept or decline his offer. Or you could pull his crown down over his eyes and run away giggling. Any of these three choices will branch the story in a different direction.

When writing for video games, using less text is often better than using more. This is because of an important game-writing rule: show, don't tell. If you can show something to players rather than simply telling it to them, always show. That way, players will feel more connected to the game's story. But before you kick back and sip on a lemonade, remember that this doesn't mean game writers can be lazy. They can't just ask the artists and the animators to do their work for them. They should write detailed descriptions of what the player sees and hears.

For example, imagine you're walking up to a spooky house in a zombie game. The writer could explain how cobwebs are hanging from the windows. He could write about the creaking walls and the zombie moans coming from the basement. After reading the script, the animators, artists, and sound designers add all of these things to the game. When the players get to the house, they will understand the house is spooky. This is much better than just having a character say, "Wow, that's a spooky house over there!" See? Show, don't tell!

Whiterun Guard

I don't have time for this...

You caught me. I'll pay you gold)

I submit. Take

In games that have branching dialogue, such as *Skyrim*, the game writer must write dialogue for every option the player might choose.

SOUND DESIGNER: Can You Hear Me Now?

Do you hear that sound? Listen very carefully ...

Hear it yet?

Can't hear anything? Well, there's a good reason for that. We haven't hired a sound designer yet. This person is in charge of literally everything you hear in a game. If it goes into your ears, the sound designer was responsible for it. That means sound effects, voices, and music. It even includes little beeping noises on the menu screens.

Once the sound designers decide what sounds they need, they have to record them. For a shooting game, they might visit a firing range and record the sounds of different gunshots. For a driving game, the sound designer might hold a microphone out of a moving car to get the sound of wheels screeching on pavement. But the sound designer's job isn't that simple. Remember that noises sound different depending on how far away you are. To make sure everything sounds right no matter where the player is standing, the sound designer records from many different distances and angles.

The sound designer also helps choose voice actors. On big-budget games, this may involve hiring famous Hollywood stars. Sound designers help the actors match their performances to the overall feel of the game. If an actor is trying to use a British accent in a game that takes place in Texas, the sound designer has to tell the actor to switch it up.

The equipment for recording and creating sound effects and music can get very complicated.

PROGRAMMER:
Writing in Code

So far, we've created a game world, figured out how characters will interact, and added sound. Now what? It's time to make all these things actually work together. It's time to call in the programmers.

Game programmers are some of the most important members of the video game team. Unfortunately, video game consoles are dumb. Really dumb. They can only follow instructions in special languages known as programming codes. And the programmers exactly what to do to make the game come to life.

There are many types of programming codes. The kind used depends on the console involved. The best programmers are familiar with many kinds of codes. Programmers must be very good at thinking logically. Remember that a game console isn't very bright. It will perfectly follow the instructions you give it—even if the instructions include a mistake. Programmers must think like a computer to fix these problems.

logically = using evidence and clear thinking to make a decision

Several kinds of programmers work on games. Some handle graphics, while others deal with sound. Physics programmers figure out how objects move within the game world. Basically, they figure out how far the *Angry Birds* will fly. Artificial-intelligence programmers decide how smart (or dumb) computer-controlled game opponents will be. Finally, the lead programmer is in charge. She or he sets up work schedules and tells the other programmers what to do.

The physics programmer for *Angry Birds* had to figure out what path the birds would take after being launched into the air.

17

Have you ever made a diorama for school? If not, here's the scoop. Basically, you use stuff like clay and paint to create a miniature scene in a small space, like a shoebox. It's a lot of fun. And think about this: the environment artist is the ultimate diorama maker.

The environment artist makes scenery and backgrounds for the game. Artists create everything from the tiny details of a single object to an entire world. Sometimes, they do both in a single game. In the game *Kerbal Space Program*, the player flies a spaceship across the galaxy. The artists had to create things as small as the bolts on the rocket engines and as huge as the moons of a planet millions of miles away. And everything in between.

The environment artist uses a computer to make three-dimensional models of all the places and objects in the game. When things are first created in the computer, they are flat and colorless. The environment artist adds colors, textures, and lighting to make the models look more interesting and realistic. For example, a desert cliff at sunset would look pretty lame if it were flat, shiny, and gray. Instead, the environment artist will tweak the lighting and textures to make it look dusty, rocky, and dramatic.

three-dimensional = having height, width, and depth

The environment artists behind *Kerbal Space Program* show players tiny details and the vast universe, all at the same time.

CHARACTER ARTIST:
What a Character!

The character artist's job is simple: **turn imagination into reality.** He or she turns characters from the game designer's imagination into detailed three-dimensional models. Just as with the environments, colors and textures must be added to make the models more realistic. Modern game consoles are powerful enough to make these models unbelievably detailed. You can see the stitching on their clothes, the individual hairs on their heads, and even the pores on their skin. Older game consoles were not powerful enough for these effects. Character models were sometimes simply covered in flat colors.

Character artists make sure the characters they create fit in with the rest of the game. If they don't fit, the result can be super weird. Imagine a dark, spooky game set in a graveyard at midnight. Then imagine a wacky cartoon rabbit bouncing around while cracking jokes. Totally out of place, right? It is the character artist's job to avoid this kind of mismatch.

Mario's original character model was extremely simple.

SPRITES

Twenty years ago, most video game consoles were not advanced enough to show three-dimensional characters and objects. Instead, two-dimensional objects were created using sprites. No, we're not talking about the soda. Sprites are images that have only height and width—no depth. Early sprites looked as though they might have been drawn on graph paper. As game consoles became more powerful, sprites became more detailed and their lines became smoother. Eventually, three-dimensional models replaced sprites for most modern games.

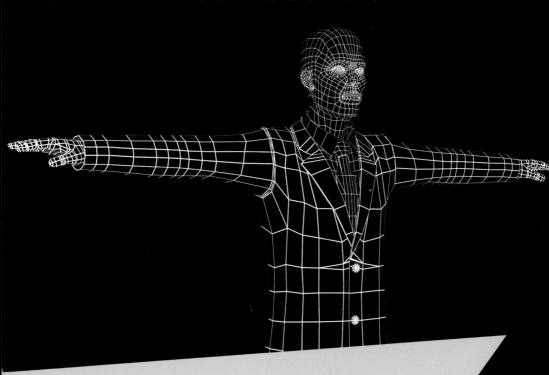

RIGGER:
Pulling the Strings

Riggers are the puppet masters of the video game world. They decide how characters and objects will move. First, the rigger turns the character artist's three-dimensional models into wire frames. Riggers take away all the detailed textures that made the characters look so lifelike. (Don't worry—the textures will be put back later.) The result is a model that looks a bit like a weird skeleton. Then the model is ready to be rigged.

wire frames =
three-dimensional models that have only lines and no surfaces

Riggers decide what parts of the model need to move. Then, they use special computer programs to place joints at the necessary points. These are just like the joints in your knees, elbows, and neck. Very detailed models may even have joints for individual fingers. Next, the rigger uses the computer to add objects known as controllers. If the rigger is the puppet master, these are the strings. The wire frame controllers allow the model to move along its joints.

Rigging sometimes includes something called motion capture. In this process, an actor wears a special suit covered in sensors that look like Ping-Pong balls. The actor acts out a game character's motions in a studio. An actor usually looks totally ridiculous while doing this. But it's all worth it. Special cameras and computers record and measure the motions. The computers use this information to create a wire-frame skeleton of the actor.

Sports stars often use motion capture to get their signature moves into a game.

L.A. NOIRE MOTION CAPTURE

The 2011 game L.A. Noire used a cool new motion capture technology called MotionScan. It allowed for amazingly realistic animation of characters' faces. The MotionScan system uses 32 cameras to capture tiny details of an actor's performance. Such detail would take tons of time and money to create by hand. The job was made much simpler by using sensors and computers.

ANIMATOR:
Putting Things in Motion

If you want to know what game animators do, think
Frankenstein without the lightning. Why?
Because animators bring video game characters to life. But there's
no way they can do it alone. They work with practically every other
person to make the animation just right. Animators work with the
game designer to decide how a character would move within the
overall game. For instance, characters in a bright, happy game
might skip or hop rather than drag their feet.

They work with the level designer to figure out how an environment will affect the character's motion. If it is raining, will characters slip and fall? And how would it look if they did? The animator also works with the combat designer to decide how characters move when they are fighting. How will a character swing a heavy sword if she is a ninja? What if he is a 10-year-old boy instead? How would the motion look different?

Animators tell a story through their animation. They help the writer show rather than tell. By working together, the animator and the writer can avoid directly saying a person is happy or it is raining. Instead, the person can walk with a little jump in his or her step and constantly smile and wave to people. The animation will make it obvious that the person is happy.

QUALITY ASSURANCE:
Testing, 1, 2, 3

Your job is to play new video games all day. They're so new, they aren't even in stores yet. No, seriously. We're not kidding. Sounds amazing, right?

Not so fast. You're not just any old gamer. You're a quality assurance (QA) tester.

Testers play video games to find problems or bugs that need to be fixed. At first, this job might sound like a piece of cake. But in reality, it involves a ton of hard work, amazing attention to detail, and incredible patience.

Testers keep stacks of notes while playing games. If something goes wrong, they must write down exactly what the problem is and what caused it. They also have to try making the problem happen again to make sure they have figured out how it happened.

The real job of testers is to break the game they're playing. What if a player tries driving the race car backward around the track? What if players fly the airplane off the game map? What if they jump onto a platform the level designer never intended them to reach? Testers must go through all the weird situations they can think of. If something goes wrong, they let the programmers know what happened. After programmers make some tweaks, the testers play that part of the game again to make sure the problem has been completely solved.

QA testing is one of the biggest entry-level jobs in the game industry. Many people begin their video game careers as testers. Skilled, hardworking testers can move on to become artists or programmers or any of the other cutting-edge people in video games. Maybe that person is you!.

QA testers work closely with programmers to find and fix problems in games.

QUICK FACTS ABOUT VIDEO GAME CAREERS

Career	Skills needed	What classes should you take?	Average Salary (2011)*
Game designer	Basic understanding of all other game careers	Game design, art, computer science	$73,386
Level designer	Computer modeling programs, graphic design	Computer science, architecture, fine art	$73,386
Combat designer	Video game knowledge, programming code	Computer science, military history, cultural studies	$73,386
Game writer	Creative writing, script writing	Literature, storytelling, fiction	$73,386

Sound designer	Audio software, recording devices	Audio technology, game design	$83,182
Programmer	Programming code, knowledge about game consoles	Computer science, game design, project management	$92,962
Environment artist	3-D modeling software, drawing, sculpting	Fine art, architecture, computer science	$75,780
Character artist	3-D modeling software, drawing, painting	Anatomy, computer science, fine art	$75,780
Rigger	Rigging software, progamming code	Animation, anatomy, computer science	$75,780
Animator	3-D animation software	Animation, anatomy, storytelling	$75,780
Quality assurance	Attention to detail, interest in games, communication skills	Computer science, basic programming	$47,910

*http://gamasutra.com/view/news/167355/Game_Developer_reveals_2011_Game_Industry_Salary_Survey_results.php

Braithwaite, Brenda, and Ian Schreiber. *Breaking into the Game Industry: Advice for a Successful Career from Those Who Have Done It*. Boston: Course Learning, 2012.
Brenda Braithwaite got her start in the video game industry when she was not much older than you are now. In this book, she shares what she has learned in her long career in gaming.

Get in Media
http://getinmedia.com/industry/games
Video game school Full Sail University has put together a great resource for people interested in a video game career. This site provides detailed, well-organized information about more than 100 different gaming careers.

How Stuff Works: Behind the Scenes
http://electronics.howstuffworks.com/3do.htm
Back when the Nintendo 64 was still around, the writers at How Stuff Works got a behind-the-scenes look at a game being made. The console may be old, but the information is still interesting and relevant today.

Interactive Achievement Awards
http://en.wikipedia.org/wiki/Interactive_Achievement_Award
To see which game makers are among the best at their jobs, check out this list of past winners of the Interactive Achievement Awards. Awards include best animation, best sound design, and game of the year.

Miller, Ron. *Digital Art: Painting with Pixels*. Minneapolis: Lerner Publications Company, 2008.
Learn about the history of digital art—the kind of art that is used to create video games. If the information you've learned about character and environment artists interests you, check out this book to take your knowledge to the next level.

Schell, Jesse. *The Art of Game Design*. Burlington, MA: Morgan Kaufmann Publishers, 2008.
This award-winning book by a college professor can do something other video game books can't—it will help you to think like a video game designer.

Video Game Careers from the Bureau of Labor Statistics
http://www.bls.gov/opub/ooq/2011/fall/art01.pdf
So you think you'd like to get into the game industry? Here's a great place to start. This government publication explains how games get made, what careers are available, and how to get a job in the game industry.

Main body text set in Calvert MT Std Regular 11/16.
Typeface provided by Monotype Typography.